THE YOUNG PRINCESS

Always a friendly and playful child (who owned 132 dolls!), Victoria was good at music, singing and dancing and was a talented artist. Her mother was German and as a child, Victoria spoke with a strong German accent. As well as English, she could also speak French and German fluently.

THE QUEEN COMES OF AGE

Princess Victoria was just 18 years old when she heard of the death of her uncle, William IV, in 1837. She was immediately filled with feelings of both happiness and sadness, but stayed calm. She was crowned the following year, on 28 June, at Westminster Abbey. She was not popular at first, but she was to become Britain's longest-reigning monarch, and rule over the greatest empire the world has ever seen.

DUCHESS OF KENT

Victoria's father was Edward, Duke of Kent, fourth son of George III. Victoria never knew her father, who died when she was a baby. Her mother, the Duchess of Kent, was appointed Regent in case Victoria succeeded to the throne whilst still a child.

PRINCE ALBERT

One of the first dilemmas facing Victoria when she succeeded to the throne was that of marriage. Lord Melbourne, the Prime Minister, advised Victoria to marry as soon as possible to create her own heirs. At first she had no interest in doing so but agreed to meet her cousin, Prince Albert of Saxe-Coburg-Gotha. Although neither of them was keen at first, they soon became very good friends. After marriage, their friendship developed into a very deep love for one another.

THE PRINCE CONSORT

Prince Albert was, in Victoria's own words, "*so sensible, so kind, and so good, and so amiable...the most pleasing and delightful exterior and appearance you can possibly see.*" He was tall, intelligent and proved to be a very good political adviser to Victoria. He took a real interest in the British, particularly the poorer classes. It is said that he re-introduced the idea of decorating trees at Christmas. This was a custom in his native Germany but had not been done in England for years.

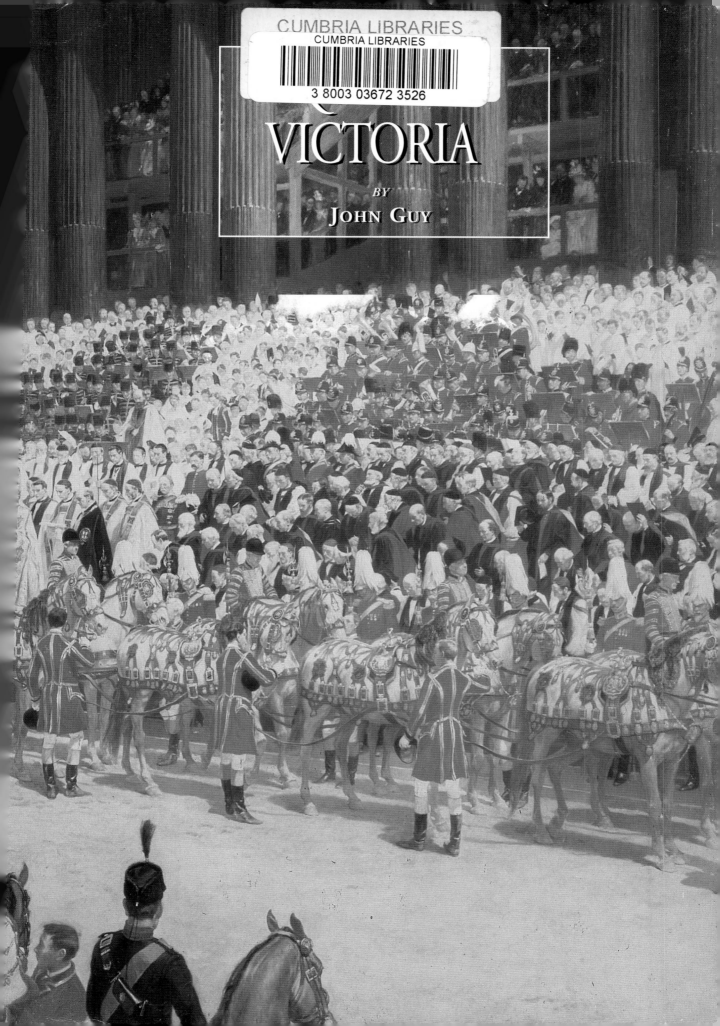

VICTORIA

BY

JOHN GUY

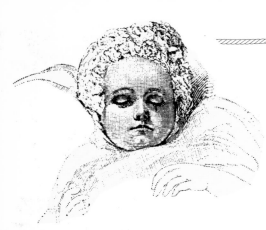

THE YOUNG VICTORIA

VICTORIA IS BORN

Victoria was born at Kensington Palace and was christened exactly one month later in the Cupola Room at the Palace. Her parents settled on Alexandrina Victoria as her registered name, but they called her Victoria from birth.

When Victoria was born on 24 Ma[...] 1819, she was fifth in line to th[...] throne. It did not seem likely tha[...] she would become queen. Her grandfather, George III, was still king and ahead of her were her uncles, George, the Prince Regent, the Dukes of York and Clarence, and her father, the Duke of Kent. However, things changed quickly. Her father died suddenly on 23 January 1820, and George III died six days later. The Duke of York died in 1827. Her other uncles succeeded as George IV and William IV but did not have any children who could succeed, so Victoria became heir to the throne.

PERSONAL POSSESSIONS

Many of Queen Victoria's personal possessions still survive, a number of them on view at the Victoria and Albert Museum. These reading glasses once belonged to her. The case is inscribed with her personal insignia.

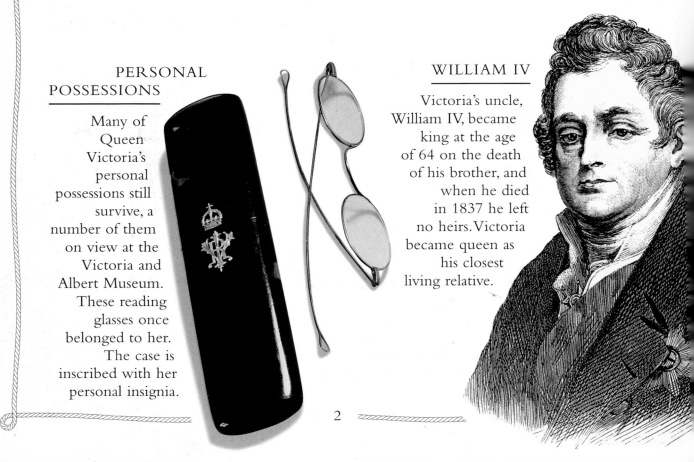

WILLIAM IV

Victoria's uncle, William IV, became king at the age of 64 on the death of his brother, and when he died in 1837 he left no heirs. Victoria became queen as his closest living relative.

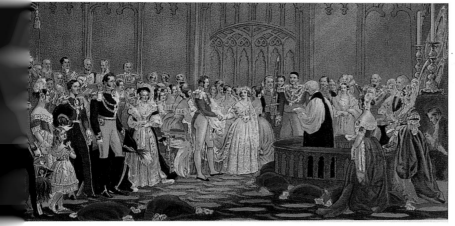

THE ROYAL WEDDING

'The wedding between Victoria and Albert took place on 10 February 1840 at St James's Palace. They were both just 20 years old. She wore a white, satin gown with a lace flounce, and a Turkish diamond necklace and sapphire brooch (a present from Albert). The couple were well received by the public. After the wedding reception held at Buckingham Palace, they had a three-day honeymoon at Windsor Castle.

THE PRINCE DIES

In 1861 Prince Albert caught typhoid fever and died at the age of 42. The queen was heartbroken. She wore black for the rest of her life out of respect for Albert. At first the public sympathized with her, but after over ten years of mourning, there were calls for her to abdicate (resign from the throne).

THE QUEEN PROPOSES

According to the rules of royal protocol, no man is allowed to propose to a queen, so Victoria had to ask for Albert's hand in marriage. She proposed to him on 15 October 1839. In her diary, Victoria wrote that Albert's acceptance was the brightest and happiest moment of her life.

KEEPSAKES

To commemorate the royal wedding a great many mementoes were made, such as this decorative lustre-ware jug.

EVENTS OF VICTORIA'S LIFE

~1819~
Victoria born at Kensington Palace

~1820~
Victoria's father Edward, Duke of Kent, dies

~1830~
George IV dies

William IV comes to the throne

~1832~
First Reform Act passed to reform parliamentary system

~1833~
Slavery abolished throughout the Empire

~1834~
Poor Law creates workhouses for the poor

Houses of Parliament burn down

~1837~
William IV dies

Victoria comes to the throne

~1838~
Victoria's coronation

People's Charter issued, calling for political reform

~1839~
First camera developed

~1840~
Victoria marries Albert of Saxe-Coburg-Gotha

FAMILY LIFE

*V*ictoria is often pictured as a stern, serious woman, and her choice to wear black for so many years after Albert's death seemed to back this up. She is rarely seen smiling in pictures, but apparently was a happy person. One reason for her glum expressions was possibly the slow film speed used by photographers at the time. Subjects often had to hold a pose for 30 seconds (or longer) so as not to blur the image, making it difficult to hold a smile. Historians have often focused on the more serious side to Victoria, forgetting about her love of life, especially family life. She was amused by her children, and both she and Albert enjoyed simple, family pastimes. In later life, Victoria loved to see herself as the great matriarch (female head of the family).

SOFTLY, SOFTLY

Contrary to popular opinion, Victoria was not very strict. She preferred to teach her children by setting a good moral example rather than to over-discipline them.

THE GRANDMOTHER OF EUROPE

This picture, taken in 1897, shows the extended family of Queen Victoria. The Prince of Wales (and future king Edward VII) stands immediately to her left. By the various marriages of her children and grandchildren, Victoria was related to all of the major royal houses of Europe, including Germany, Norway, Sweden, Greece, Spain, Romania and Russia, earning her the affectionate title 'the grandmother of Europe'.

HAPPY FAMILIES

In keeping with most families of the day, Victoria and Albert had many children, nine in all. She gave birth to Princess Victoria (Vicky) in November 1840. Vicky, the Princess Royal, remained a close friend throughout the queen's life, especially after Albert's death. Victoria's family life was a happy one. It is difficult to say what kind of relationship she had with all her children: some accounts claim she was rather cold, others paint a warmer picture. There were problems between her and Edward, the future king. She thought he was foolish and often criticized his behaviour.

PERSONAL RECOLLECTIONS

We know a great deal about the personal life and opinions of Queen Victoria from her diary, which she kept throughout her life. It was not a secret diary. In her younger years it was frequently read by her mother and governess.

EVENTS OF VICTORIA'S LIFE

~1840~
Penny Postal service introduced

Princess 'Vicky' born (Victoria's first child)

~1841~
Sir Robert Peel becomes Prime Minister

~1845~
Beginning of Irish potato famine

~1846~
Corn Laws repealed

~1851~
Great Exhibition in London, initiated by Prince Albert

~1853~
Vaccination against smallpox made compulsory

Albert begins rebuilding Balmoral Castle to his own designs

~1854~
Crimean War breaks out between Britain (and France) and Russia

~1856~
Victoria Cross first introduced for bravery in wartime

~1857~
Indian Mutiny against British rule

ASSASSINATION ATTEMPTS

At the beginning of her reign Queen Victoria was not popular. As ruling monarch, she was often seen as the cause of social problems; some would have preferred a king on the throne. There were several attempts made on Victoria's life including this attempt in 1840 by Edward Oxford.

REFORM ACTS

During her reign, Victoria approved several important Acts of Parliament. New political movements were calling for change. In 1838 the Chartists issued the 'Peoples' Charter', which demanded political reform. Although not fully developed until 1944, it forms the basis of our parliamentary system today. In 1867 and 1884, the Second and Third Reform Acts extended the right to vote to more people.

FATHER FIGURE

During the early years of her reign Victoria relied heavily on the advice of Lord Melbourne, the Whig (Liberal) Prime Minister (left). He guided her through the complications of politics and her role in government.

SOCIAL CHANGE

The Industrial Revolution saw Britain change from farming to industry. People who left the country to find work in the towns were taken advantage of by greedy industrialists. Trade unionists such as Joseph Arch, founder of the National Union of Farm Labourers (shown right), fought a long and hard battle for workers' rights. Trade unions were finally legalized in 1871.

VICTORIA'S GOVERNMENT

From the beginning, Victoria showed a real interest in the government of the country and developed a good relationship with most of the leading politicians of the day. She accepted the relatively new idea of a constitutional monarchy (which meant that she had no real part to play in politics), but she realized that she had considerable influence and used her powers wisely. Albert also took an active role in matters of government.

POLITICAL GIANTS

Victoria witnessed the coming and going of several great politicians, including William Gladstone and Benjamin Disraeli (above). Victoria liked Disraeli and had him made Earl of Beaconsfield, whereas Gladstone often angered her.

A NEW HOUSE FOR PARLIAMENT

Until the reign of Victoria's uncle, William IV, Parliament met in the old royal palace of Westminster. Like most medieval buildings, it contained a lot of wood and burned down in a terrible fire in 1834. The present Houses of Parliament were rebuilt on part of the old palace site. Victoria attended the opening of the new building in 1867.

LIFE EXPECTANCY

This picture shows a father comforting his dying child. Childhood deaths were not uncommon in Victorian Britain. There was no National Health Service, and the poor could rarely afford medical treatment. In the country the life expectancy was around 50, but for those living in bad conditions in towns many were lucky to reach 40.

SMALLPOX

One of the most contagious and deadly diseases was smallpox. The scientist, Edward Jenner, developed a vaccine to combat the disease. Vaccination was made compulsory in 1853.

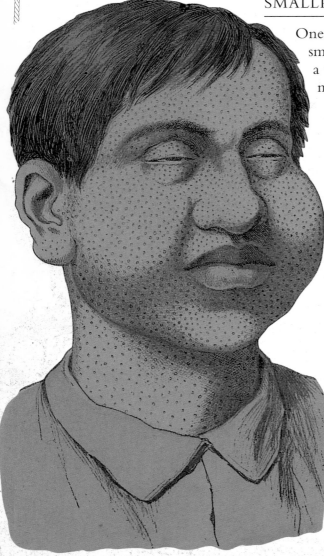

SANITATION

Many of the diseases common in Victorian Britain were caused through poor sanitation and living conditions. A series of Public Health Acts after 1848 made it the responsibility of local councils to provide proper drainage and clean water supplies.

Only the rich could afford the luxury of an indoor toilet. The poor had to make do with open cesspits in the backyard or, worse still, a communal toilet shared by up to 100 others.

LIFE IN VICTORIAN ENGLAND

No proper postal service had existed in Britain until 1840 when the Penny Post was introduced. This revolutionized the delivery of letters, and for just 1d. (0.4p) a letter could be sent anywhere in the country. The first stamp issued was the Penny Black. It carried a profile of the queen, a tradition adopted throughout the empire and still maintained today.

At the beginning of Victoria's reign (1837), the population of Britain was about 20 million, only 20 percent of whom lived in towns. The rest still managed to make a living from the land. By the end of her reign (1901) the population had doubled, with over 75 percent living in towns. These growing populations meant that row upon row of poor-quality terraced slums were built around the factories. Living conditions were bad, and there were diseases, especially waterborne diseases such as cholera and typhoid.

WORKHOUSES

Workhouses were first introduced in 1834 and were often the only help available for the poor and homeless in Victorian towns. People received basic food and lodging in return for work, often in extremely harsh conditions.

SOCIAL HISTORIAN

Charles Dickens (1812–70) was the greatest and most popular novelist of his day. Many of his novels, such as *Oliver Twist*, paint a vivid description of life in Victorian Britain and he was often seen as a champion of the poor. Victoria started to accept Dickens's picture of Britain when her own beloved husband died of typhoid, probably caught from the open sewers around Windsor.

ART FOR ART'S SAKE

Both Victoria and Charles Dickens spoke out against the Pre-Raphaelite movement in art. The Pre-Raphaelites were a group of young artists (including Millais, whose painting *The Bridesmaid* is shown above) who rejected the artistic 'establishment' and classical themes.

ART AND INVENTIONS

The speed at which new inventions and discoveries appeared in Victorian Britain was very fast. These developments changed the way people had been living almost overnight. The first electric light bulbs were invented in America by Thomas Edison who, in 1877, also invented the phonograph (forerunner of modern hi-fi). The telephone was invented in 1875 by a Scotsman, Alexander Graham Bell. Food processing and packaging in tins kept food fresh for longer. Many items, however, were still expensive and enjoyed only by the rich.

PHOTOGRAPHIC RECORD

Victoria's was the first reign in history to be fully documented in photographs. The first primitive photographic images were produced in 1800. The first camera, as shown here, was developed by William Fox Talbot in 1839.

THE MEDICINE MEN

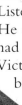

The Victorian Age was a period of great learning, when great minds worked together to push the bounds of human knowledge to the limits. Doctors such as Joseph Lister (left) recognized that bacteria were the cause of infection. He developed an antiseptic in 1867. Before that, chloroform had been developed for use as an anaesthetic during operations. Victoria herself was given chloroform during the birth of her last child, Beatrice, in 1857.

ARTISTIC LICENCE

It has often been said that the Victorians did not have an architectural style of their own, but merely borrowed from the past. In fact, their use of cast iron and glass was 'Victorian'. In more traditional buildings they borrowed a variety of styles, such as medieval, to create 'Victorian Gothic', as seen here at Cardiff Castle.

GRANDIOSE IDEAS

The Victorians built on a big scale. They built the largest buildings then known, reflecting the confidence of the new industrial age. The use of cast iron and glass made it possible to span huge floor areas. This view shows the railway station at St Pancras under construction.

EVENTS OF VICTORIA'S LIFE

~1859~
Charles Darwin publishes *On the Origin of Species*

~1861~
Prince Albert dies of typhoid

Victoria goes into mourning and withdraws from public life

~1863~
Edward, Prince of Wales (Victoria's eldest son and heir) marries Alexandra of Denmark

~1867~
Canada becomes first country within British Empire to be declared an independent dominion

Second Reform Bill passed; further parliamentary reforms

New Houses of Parliament opened

~1868~
William Gladstone becomes Prime Minister

AGE OF SCIENCE

Michael Faraday's experiments with electro-magnetism led to electricity becoming a major power source. Eager to promote the use of new technologies, Queen Victoria had electric lighting installed in all her palaces. She also demonstrated this new technology during her Diamond Jubilee celebrations in 1897 by pressing an electric button that was connected to a telegraph. It sent a message throughout the empire, beginning the tradition of the royal broadcast on Christmas Day.

THE GREAT EXHIBITION

JOSEPH PAXTON

The Crystal Palace building was designed by Joseph Paxton, a brilliant engineer and this was his masterpiece. It was truly a wonder of the age and Queen Victoria called it a 'fairy-tale palace'. Paxton received £5,000 (which is the equivalent of £1 million today) for designing and building it.

The Great Exhibition of 1851 was the idea of Prince Albert. He thought an international exhibition in London would both act as a 'shop window' for British industry, and result in more work for the poor. The government was not keen but Albert won public support and private finance through the press. The exhibition was opened on 1 May 1851 by Queen Victoria and was a great success. From then until it closed on 15 October, over six million people visited the exhibition (Britain's population was only about 20 million). It was the world's first international trade exhibition.

PREFABRICATED BUILDING

The Crystal Palace, shown here during its original construction, was made of prefabricated parts which enabled the building to be taken down after the exhibition closed in Hyde Park and rebuilt at Sydenham in 1854. The area is still known as Crystal Palace. Sadly, the building burned down in a huge fire in 1936.

FROM FAR AND WIDE

Inside the exhibition building there were over 14,000 different exhibitors, over half of whom were from the British Empire. Industrialists from across the globe came to view the best of British industry.
They placed orders for all sorts of things, from steam trains to spinning machines, textiles to fine art. Entry fees were reduced after two days to allow the public to attend.

MUSEUMS FOR ALL

Albert wanted the ordinary people of Britain to benefit from the exhibition. Money raised was used to open several large museums in London. These included the Victoria and Albert, the Science, and the Natural History Museums, which were admired worldwide.

THE CRYSTAL PALACE

The original exhibition building at Hyde Park, was a masterpiece of cast iron and glass, earning it the title 'The Crystal Palace'.
It covered an area of 105,000 square metres and was three times the size of St Paul's Cathedral. It was about 550 metres long and contained over 300,000 panes of glass.

WORKSHOP OF THE WORLD

MAN OF GENIUS

Throughout the Victorian era there were many brilliant men. Isambard Kingdom Brunel was one of these. A clever engineer, he specialized in the use of iron and steel in his designs for ships and engineering projects. His revolutionary liner, the *Great Britain,* was launched by Prince Albert in 1843; at that time it was the biggest ship ever built.

The Victorians believed that work was a virtue and good for the soul – none more than Victoria herself. Technological developments were faster in Britain than anywhere else in the world. Britain had been the first to take on the new 'industrial revolution' sweeping the developed countries, earning it the title 'Workshop of the World'.

WORKING CONDITIONS

The working class suffered because of rapid industrialization. People used to farming now had to work in mines and factories, often some distance away from their homes and in cramped and airless conditions.

THE PRICE OF PROGRESS

One of the worst parts of town life was the pollution that came from burning large quantities of fossil fuels, such as coal. Victoria increasingly found life in London unbearable and spent long periods in the country.

CHILD LABOUR

Women and children were used to working on farms, but in industrial Britain they were forced to work long hours in very poor conditions. Fourteen hours a day was quite usual and factory owners would employ children as young as five.

WHEEL OF FORTUNE

Both Britain and the empire benefited from industrialization. British industries sold their goods to the colonies. In turn, the colonies provided the raw materials for Britain to make more goods. Britain built up a large merchant fleet to transport these goods, and the British navy protected the ships and became the largest in the world.

RAILWAYS

At the beginning of Victoria's reign there were about 3,200 kilometres of railway in Britain. By 1870 this figure had grown to 22,000 kilometres. At first the railways were not popular, especially among canal owners, but 'railway mania' soon took over. Branch lines opened up all over the country, transporting goods cheaply and quickly from the factories to the ports.

FIRST COLONIES

The British Empire began as a small collection of colonies along the eastern coast of North America. They formed themselves into 13 states and became independent in the reign of Victoria's grandfather, George III. Colonies were also set up in what is now Canada during a search for a north-west passage to Asia.

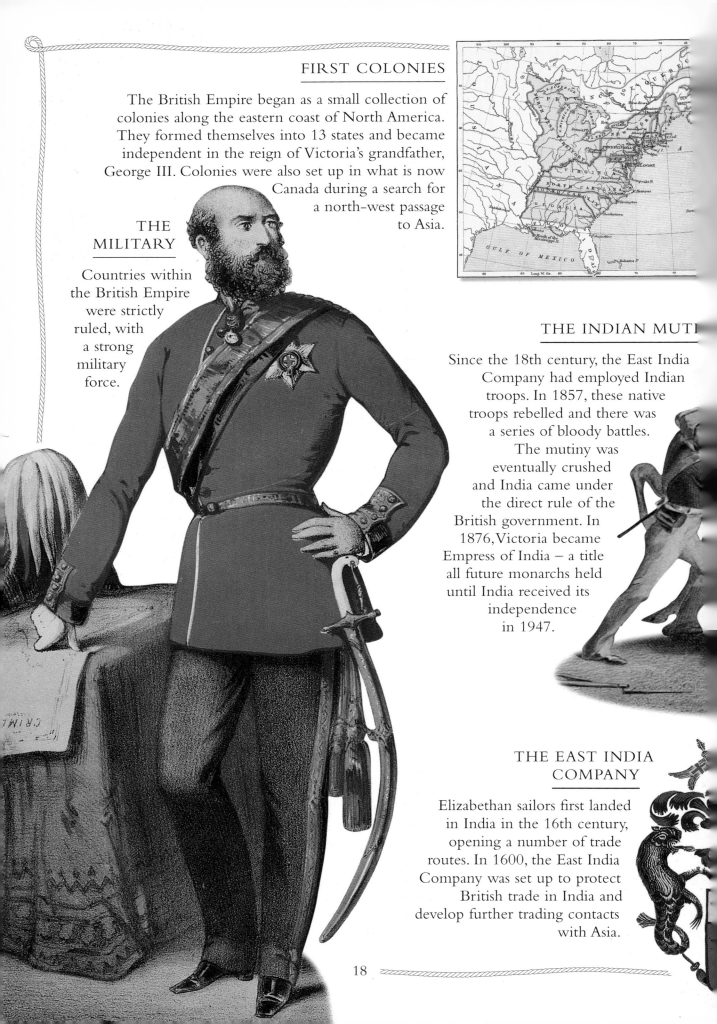

THE MILITARY

Countries within the British Empire were strictly ruled, with a strong military force.

THE INDIAN MUTINY

Since the 18th century, the East India Company had employed Indian troops. In 1857, these native troops rebelled and there was a series of bloody battles. The mutiny was eventually crushed and India came under the direct rule of the British government. In 1876, Victoria became Empress of India – a title all future monarchs held until India received its independence in 1947.

THE EAST INDIA COMPANY

Elizabethan sailors first landed in India in the 16th century, opening a number of trade routes. In 1600, the East India Company was set up to protect British trade in India and develop further trading contacts with Asia.

THE BRITISH EMPIRE

By the end of Victoria's reign she had the largest empire that the world had ever seen. Always conscious of her position, Victoria created the 'family of nations', later known as the Commonwealth. Unlike other past empires, Britain's interests lay with trade and the wealth it generated, rather than world domination. Although helped by the military, the empire gained colonies in a piecemeal way, all over the world.

ORIGINS OF THE EMPIRE

The origins of the British Empire can be traced to the reign of Elizabeth I. In Elizabeth's time, England was often at war with other European nations, particularly Spain which controlled all the major trade routes to the Americas and the East. A series of voyages to uncharted areas of the world became quests for new trade routes and land to set up new colonies.

ROBERT CLIVE

Britain's rule in India began with the victory of Robert Clive in 1757. He defeated the massive combined Indo-French army of 60,000 with a small force of 3,000 men, taking the province of Bengal. Although regarded as a hero back in Britain, Clive was understandably hated by the Indians.

EXTENT OF THE EMPIRE

This map shows the extent of the British Empire (coloured orange) in 1886. All of the major trading routes were under British control, which is why Britain was such a major influence throughout the world.

BRITISH WAY OF LIFE

When taking control of a new land, Britain forced the native people to adopt British ways. Official buildings and houses were built in British styles and British legal and government systems were introduced. The English language became widely spoken and remains the most spoken language in the world.

EQUAL PORTIONS

Throughout the 18th and 19th centuries there was considerable 'land-hunger' amongst the major world powers. They thought that the world was theirs for the taking and did not consider the native peoples. This cartoon shows various heads of state dividing up China like pieces of pie, while the Chinese leader looks on helplessly.

NEW COLONIES

The British Empire grew slowly. At its largest it covered a quarter of the world's landmass. It reached its peak immediately after the First World War, when the former German colonies in Africa and Asia were taken over. Because its colonies were scattered across the world, the empire became impossible to govern. The military were unable to cope and when Britain began to have economic problems at home, the empire began to decline.

FLYING THE FLAG

The raising of the Union Jack showed British sovereignty over a newly acquired country. It was always accompanied by much pomp and ceremony.

VOYAGES OF DISCOVERY

In Elizabethan times, the reasons for exploration were quite simple: gold and new trade routes. By Victoria's reign, it was normal for explorers to take scientists with them on their voyages, to record and bring back samples of new plants and animal species for scientific study. This practice was started by explorers such as James Cook who is seen here raising the Union Jack in New South Wales, Australia, in 1770.

THE GOLDEN ERA

"NEW CROWNS FOR OLD ONES!"

EMPRESS OF INDIA

In 1876 Queen Victoria was named Empress of India and was proud to accept the title. She is seen in this cartoon, being asked by Prime Minister Disraeli to trade the imperial crown of India for her own.

The reign of Victoria was a golden era, a time when even the queen herself believed that the "sun would never set on the Empire". It was also a period of great social and economic change, when Britain led the world in science and technology. Although the British government exploited the colonies, many of them benefited from Britain's developments. Many of the world's railway systems, for example, were built by British engineers, and items manufactured in Britain were exported all over the globe. In short, Britain took the world by storm.

FRESH START

One of the strengths of the British Empire lay in colonizing the nations it controlled with British citizens. These emigrants, bound for Australia, were keen to start a new life in the colonies, away from the poverty and unemployment at home.

THE GERMAN THREAT

The main threat to the empire came from Victoria's own grandson, Germany's Kaiser Wilhelm II. Although Britain's navy was the greatest in the world, Germany was able to build modern warships at a faster rate than Britain could replace its out-of-date ones.

BRITANNIA RULES THE WAVES

Four days after Victoria's Diamond Jubilee in 1897, the Royal Navy put on a massive display of power at Spithead, on the south coast. It was the largest collection of warships ever assembled and demonstrated to the world the power of the British Empire.

SLAVERY ABOLISHED

Slavery was abolished throughout the empire in 1833, some years before Victoria's reign. The treatment of native peoples from the colonies was a matter close to the queen's heart. She was against giving the Boers of South Africa their independence, for example, fearing they would treat the natives too harshly.

Le Petit Journal
SUPPLÉMENT · ILLUSTRÉ

ÉVÉNEMENTS DU TRANSVAAL
Sommation aux Anglais

BADEN-POWELL

Lieutenant-Colonel Robert Baden-Powell became a national hero during the Boer War. He held the small South African trading post of Mafeking against 8,000 Boers. He had just 1,000 soldiers and lost only 35 men. Baden-Powell went on to form the Boy Scout movement in 1908.

BRITAIN AT WAR

Throughout Victoria's reign, as Britain greatly extended its empire, there were a number of conflicts. With rising unemployment at home, there was no shortage of manpower to join the ranks of the army. Like Britain, all the other major powers in Europe were keen to get new colonies. This wish to empire-build led to one of the worst conflicts in history: the First World War.

THE BOER WAR (1899-1902)

The Boers were South African farmers descended from Dutch settlers. They fiercely resisted Britain's attempts to take over South Africa after the discovery of gold there. They used guerrilla tactics to fight the massive British force sent against them. Eventually though the size of the British Army overwhelmed them and they were defeated.

THE CRIMEAN WAR (1854–56)

The Crimean War was fought between Britain and Russia on a peninsula that is now part of modern-day Turkey. Britain was unprepared for the scale of the conflict. It led to one of its worst military disasters – the 'Charge of the Light Brigade', at Balaclava in 1854.

W. NORMAN, (PRIVATE) BRINGING IN SINGLE-HANDED TWO RUSSIAN PRISONERS.

THOMAS BEACH (PRIVATE) AT INKERMAN, RESCUING COLONEL CARPENTER.

F. C. ELTON (MAJOR) WORKING IN THE TRENCHES UNDER A HEAVY FIRE.

FLORENCE NIGHTINGALE

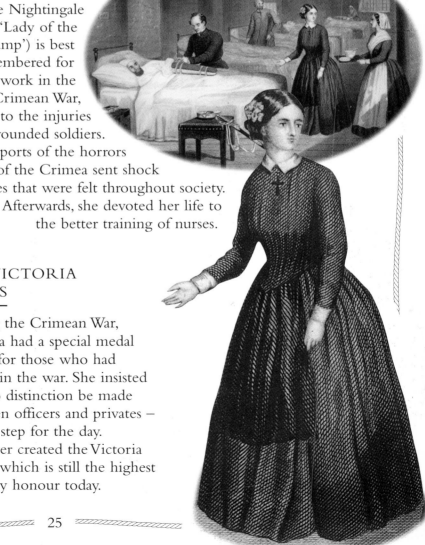

Florence Nightingale (the 'Lady of the Lamp') is best remembered for her work in the Crimean War, tending to the injuries of wounded soldiers. Her reports of the horrors of the Crimea sent shock waves that were felt throughout society. Afterwards, she devoted her life to the better training of nurses.

THE VICTORIA CROSS

During the Crimean War, Victoria had a special medal struck for those who had served in the war. She insisted that no distinction be made between officers and privates – a bold step for the day. She later created the Victoria Cross, which is still the highest military honour today.

THE ROYAL PALACES

Victoria and Albert made full use of the royal palaces. For official duties, balls and government functions they favoured Buckingham Palace (shown here in 1852), but the queen always preferred the privacy of Windsor Castle. As a young girl Victoria enjoyed the hurly-burly of London's social scene, but Albert preferred the peace and quiet of the country estates. Later in life, Victoria also came to prefer them.

BUCKINGHAM PALACE

The population census of 1841 shows Buckingham Palace to be Queen Victoria's main home. It is still the residence most often associated with British royalty, but is quite new to the list of royal palaces. Victoria's grandfather, George III, bought the house for £28,000 in 1762. The state apartments are magnificent, and frequently host state functions.

...NE HOUSE

In 1844, Victoria and Albert began looking for a house to retire to. The Osborne estate on the Isle of Wight proved ideal, and Prince Albert designed the house in Italian Renaissance style.

BALMORAL CASTLE

This view shows part of Victoria's private apartments (the drawing room) at Balmoral Castle in Scotland. Surrounded by mountains and set in 121,000 square kilometres of deer forest, Balmoral has always been a royal favourite since it was bought and redesigned by Prince Albert in 1853.

WINDSOR CASTLE

Windsor Castle is the oldest royal residence in Britain and also the largest inhabited castle in the world. Begun by William the Conqueror in 1066 it has been greatly extended since then. All monarchs up to George IV, Victoria's uncle, continued to transform the great medieval castle into a grand palace.

THE JUBILEE YEARS

*T*he last years of Victoria's reign were very different from the early years. Although she eventually came out of mourning for Albert 13 years after his death (in 1874), she never got over his loss. She returned to public life, but with advancing years the queen became a sadder person. Victoria had not always been popular during her reign. Many had not welcomed her to the throne, but by the time of her Golden Jubilee in 1887 she was at the height of her popularity.

NEVER-TO-BE-FORGOTTEN DAY

The Queen's Golden Jubilee marked 50 years of her reign. People throughout the empire celebrated the event, particularly in Britain itself (and more especially in London) with wild enthusiasm. Victoria said of the occasion: "*This never-to-be-forgotten day will always leave the most gratifying and heart-stirring memories behind.*"

FAMILY GATHERING

On the occasion of her Golden Jubilee, Victoria attended a banquet held in her honour in Buckingham Palace. Invited guests included all the crowned heads of Europe, most of whom were related to Victoria. For her Diamond Jubilee in 1897, as this portrait shows, the gathering was of her 'extended family' from countries throughout the empire.

THE DIAMOND JUBILEE

This painting shows Queen Victoria arriving at St Paul's Cathedral for a service on 22 June 1897 in honour of her Diamond Jubilee. Out of respect for her age and poor health the service was short.

ROYAL INVITE

This picture shows one of the formal invitations to the Queen's Diamond Jubilee celebrations at the Guildhall in London. This was one of many public functions held throughout the country. By this time Victoria was a frail old lady confined to a wheelchair. However, she continued to perform her duties right up until a few weeks before she died.

THE END OF AN ERA

FAMILY FEUDS

This family tree shows that most of Victoria's children married into the royal houses of Europe. She hoped this would have a stabilizing effect on European politics. Sadly, this was not to be.

The end of an era came with the death of Victoria on 22 January 1901. She had many sides to her character. She took a keen interest in improving the living conditions of the poor, but did not approve of women taking a profession. However, she was concerned about the working conditions of women and children in factories and mines. She was against giving the vote to women, but agreed that working-class men should have the vote. Britain had seen more change during her reign than in any other period of history.

THREAT TO PEACE

This picture shows the Kaiser, Wilhelm II, Victoria's grandson by marriage. Victoria always disliked his anti-British views, but he was at her bedside when she lay dying. Had she lived a few more years she would have seen him lead Germany against Britain in the First World War.

PROBLEM CHILD

This view shows Victoria with her son, the future King Edward VII, shortly before her death. She was always critical of Edward and did not think he would make a good king. She kept him out of government matters because she feared he might create problems. In later life she finally accepted him as her heir.

TRUSTED ADVISER

Victoria was a very moral person but she was also linked to scandal. When she was mourning Albert she became friendly with a Scottish servant, John Brown. He was a superb rider and Victoria trusted him. He became a constant companion, and there were rumours that they were having an affair. This caused Victoria's popularity to decline.

FAMILY PORTRAIT

This family portrait was taken at Osborne House in 1898, three years before Victoria's death. When she died, her body was taken from there to Cowes and on to London. Her funeral was carried out according to her own instructions and she was buried at Frogmore, in the Home Park of Windsor Castle. She was buried with her beloved husband, Prince Albert.

EVENTS OF VICTORIA'S LIFE

~1887~
Independent Labour Party founded

~1897~
Victoria's Diamond Jubilee celebrates 60 years on the throne

Spithead naval review

~1899~
Boer War breaks out in South Africa

~1900~
Victoria's son, Alfred, dies

~1901~
Queen Victoria dies

Edward VII comes to the throne

GLOSSARY

Anaesthetic Something that reduces a person's ability to feel pain. Before this was invented, all operations were carried out with the patient wide awake.

Antiseptic Something that stops the growth of bacteria which can cause infections and disease.

Census An official survey of the public. This can include information about population size, where people live and many other things.

Chloroform A type of anaesthetic popular in Victorian times.

Cholera A serious infectious disease which affects the intestines. It is caused by eating or drinking something infected with the bacteria.

Guerrilla A type of warfare carried out by small groups. It is often very difficult for regular armies to fight guerrilla groups.

Piecemeal Achieving something by small acts over a long period of time rather than a single act.

Prefabricated A building that is made in sections and therefore easy to assemble.

Protocol An official set of rules that set out how to behave in certain circumstances.

Typhoid A serious infectious disease which causes a fever, red spots over the chest, and severe pain. It is caused by bacteria and was often deadly at this time.

Vaccination A treatment that makes someone immune (not affected by) to a particular disease.

ACKNOWLEDGEMENTS

We would like to thank: Graham Rich, Rosie Hankin and Elizabeth Wiggans for their assistance and David Hobbs for his map of the world.
Copyright © 2008 *ticktock* Entertainment Ltd.
Published by *ticktock* Media Ltd, Unit 2, Orchard Business Centre North Farm Road, Tunbridge Wells, Kent TN2 3XF, U.K.
All rights reserved. No part of this publication may be reproduced, stored in a retrieval system, or transmitted in any form or by any means electronic, mechanical, photocopying, recording or otherwise, without prior written permission of the copyright owner.
A CIP catalogue record for this book is available from the British Library.
ISBN 978 1 84696 659 0
Picture research by Image Select.
Printed in China.

Picture Credits:
t=top, b=bottom, c=centre, l=left, r=right, OFC=outside front cover, IFC=inside front cover, OBC=outside back cover, IBC=inside back cover

Ann Ronan at Image Select International Ltd; OBC - right, 2tl, 2br, 4r, 5c, 6bl, 6tl, 8tr, 8c, 9tr, 9bl & OFC, 10bl & OBC, 10br, 10t, 11br, 11tr & OBC, 12bl, 13br, 13c, 14tl, 14bl, 16br, 16tl & OBC, 16/17c & OFC, 17t, 17br, 18l, 18/19c, 19tr, 21b, 22b, 22tl, 23tl, 23tr, 24bl, 24/25cb, 25cr & 25br, 30tl, 31tr. The Bridgeman Art Library, London; OBC - bottom left, 3br, 3tl, 3t, 4l & OFC, 5bl, 7tl, 8bl, 11cb, 12tl, 13tl, 15tl, 16bl, 18/19cb, 20t, 20bl, 23bl & 23br, 26/27 (main image), 27tr, 28bl & OFC (main image), 28tl & OFC, 29cl, 30/31c. Bridgeman - Giraudon; IFC & 29tr. Chris Fairclough Colour Library at Image Select International Ltd; 9br, 27c. The Fotomas Index (London); 2bl, 6/7cb, 19br. By Courtesy of Fine Art Photographic Library; 25t. Image Select International Ltd; 12/13c, 14/15c, 18tr,, 26tl, 30/31cb, 30bl. Mary Evans Picture Library, London; 5tl, 15br, 20br & OFC, 24tl, 32c & OFC, 26/27c, 29b. Spectrum Colour Library; 21tr.

Every effort has been made to trace the copyright holders and we apologise in advance for any unintentional omissions.
We would be pleased to insert the appropriate acknowledgement in any subsequent edition of this publication.